Hokusai

Matthi Forrer

BARNES
&NOBLE
BOOKS
NEW YORK

Katsushika Hokusai

Matthi Forrer, *conservator at the National Museum of Ethnology, Leyden, Holland.*

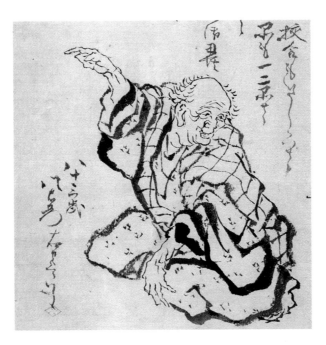

Artist's self-portrait at 83 years old.

Paper and Ink drawing, appearing in a letter (269 x 169 mm; 10.59 x 6.65 inches), signed: Old Hachiemon at 83 years; chop: Manji, 1842.
Leiden, National Museum of Ethnology.

Katsushika Hokusai (1760-1849) is undoubtedly one of Japan's best-known artists, both in Japan and in the Western world. Though his name may not always be recognized, some of his woodcuts are so familiar that they have become cultural icons, which today find their way into advertising, logos and even cartoons. His Great Wave is widely recognized as a Japanese masterpiece, and his series, Thirty-six Views of Mount Fuji, done when he was in his seventies, has undoubtedly contributed to the universal fame of this prestigious mountain. Hokusai is generally regarded as Japan's foremost landscape artist. His nearest rival, Hiroshige (1797-1858), completed his series, Fifty-three Stations of the Tokaido Road, three years after the publication of Hokusai's Fuji series, while still a young man in his thirties.

Hokusai was born in 1760 in the Honjo district of Japan's capital, Edo, on the east bank of the Sumida River, an area formerly part of Katsushika County. Although the records indicate that he was born on the 23rd day of the ninth month in the lunar calendar used in Japan at the time, it would be of more importance to the artist himself that he was born in the zodiacal Year of the Dragon. About his youth, little is known. Born to the Kawamura family, he was known by the name of Tokitaro. There is some speculation that Hokusai was the illegitimate son of Nakajima Iso, a mirror-polisher at the court of the Shogun, who adopted him as a child. Despite his presumed relation to Nakajima Iso, Hokusai was apparently never brought into in the family business, but instead was employed in a lending library in his teens. His job, common in the numerous lending libraries in existence at that time, was probably to deliver popular novels to the library's clients. Around the age of fourteen, he was apprenticed to a sculpture studio, and began learning to carve the blocks with which the popular illustrated novels and woodcut prints were reproduced. However, his real passion, as he later stated on several occasions, was drawing: "By the age of six, I was already drawing all kinds of things", wrote Hokusai in 1834.

In 1778, then in his late teens, Hokusai was admitted to the most prestigious portrait studio of the period, led by Katsukawa Shunsho (1726-1793). This studio specialized in the portraits of kabuki actors. His first woodcuts, appearing in 1779, were signed Shunro, a name bestowed upon him by his new master, but they were crudely carved and badly printed, not at all on the same level as the work produced by his master and the senior apprentices in the studio, notably Shunko, Shunjo and Shunei. Like most apprentices, he was probably assigned the projects destined for the mass market of undiscriminating buyers satisfied with cheap reproductions at a low price. Very few of the hundreds of woodcuts that Hokusai must have carved during this period have survived, and they have at best curiosity value, providing as they do an example of his early work. It was not until 1791, when the important publisher Tsutaya Juzaburo decided to give the apprentice a chance, that several pieces of artistic value were printed, and well printed at that. But by this point in time, Hokusai had apparently lost interest in the world of actor portraiture and had begun looking for other challenges.

Hokusai seems to have disappeared from the art world for a period of time; from 1792 to 1796, he produced very little, mostly illustrations for popular novels. He is said to have taken lessons from a Kano-school painter and he almost certainly spent some time studying Western styles of painting. Certain researchers, trying to explain his relative absence from the art scene during this time, identify Hokusai with the mysterious actor portraitist, Sharaku, whose work appeared only from 1794 to 1795. The beginning of 1796 marked the reappearance of the Year of the Dragon and, with its arrival, Hokusai, now using the name Hokusai Sori, resurfaced to complete a number of privately issued woodcuts. These prints, called egoyomi if they contain calendar information and surimono if they present an image accompanied by poetry, were mainly issued in honor of the New Year and were distributed among friends, with no commercial intent. The well-to-do amateur poets responsible for these prints encouraged the development of this relatively new kind of deluxe woodcut, which were sometimes issued as small books presenting a variety of styles unconnected to the traditional subjects of the ukiyoe school, such as kabuki actors or beautiful courtesans, to mention but two of this school's principal themes.

Hokusai's first treatment of the Wave theme which would eventually bring him lasting fame appeared in one of these deluxe picture books, Yanagi no ito, printed for the New Year of 1797. A comparison of this printed plate and a painting by Shiba Kokan (1747-1818), known to have been first exhibited in an Edo temple in 1793, reveals such a startling similarity that it seems obvious Hokusai was inspired by Kokan's painting. Hokusai returned to this theme several times at the turn of the century, until, finally in 1830, he produced the majestic Great Wave. His illustrations for other similar picture books and his other surimono woodcuts represent much more intimate scenes, mainly situated in the outskirts of the capital, as opposed to the better known backdrops of the city center.

Hokusai's familiarity with the world of poets and writers probably helped ensure him a number of commissions during this period. These commissioned paintings portray the beautiful faces of women which are now associated with his "Sori period". Most of this work was executed on paper, in ink and a few light colors; many of the paintings were paired with poems by well-known writers of the day. Most likely, they were produced almost casually at the cultural events to which Hokusai was invited as a matter of course, now that he had become one of the cultural elite.

It is not only his contributions to the deluxe picture books issued by and for the cultural elite of Edo which confirm his rise to fame, less than ten years after giving up his career as a portraitist of Kabuki actors. His status as an independent artist is further corroborated by the "map" of the ukiyoe world, drawn by the writer Shikitei Sanha (1776-1822): islands representing individuals, including Kitagawa, Utamaro, Sharaku and Hokusai, are surrounded by clusters which represent the Utagawaî, Kitso, and Katsukawa traditions, to name a few of the various traditions in the world of Japanese woodcuts. More explicit proof of his fame comes from a number of prestigious paintings, mostly of courtesans. These paintings are executed on silk and make use of the full palette of colors available to the artist. They were apparently commissioned by rich merchants, most likely the patrons of the high-class courtesans of the Yoshiwara.

At the beginning of the nineteenth century, Hokusai began to explore two new directions in his art. First, he became actively involved in the illustration of the serial novels popular at the time. Some of these novels were very long, and were published over long periods, occasionally up to thirty years. In his illustrations, Hokusai experimented with incorporating Chinese elements into his otherwise very Japanese compositions. In many cases, his imaginative artwork contributed greatly to the success of the novel.

The second direction explored seriously by Hokusai in the early nineteenth century was the use of perspective and the effects of chiaroscuro as employed in Western painting. By adopting an unusual viewpoint, or adding clear cast shadows and Western-style cloud formations, elements almost totally absent in the majority of Japanese woodcuts, he managed to produce surprisingly innovative landscapes of well known scenes of Edo. To further enhance the Western aspect of these landscapes, Hokusai added decorated picture frames and even went so far as to indicate the woodcut's title and to sign his name in horizontal script. Two series of five plates were produced in this manner, and despite of the small

format of the paper chosen, they constituted a deluxe edition beyond the means of many. In fact, given the absence of a publisher's mark, they may even have been distributed privately.

The plates mentioned above were not the first of Hokusai's experiments with Western styles, though they are possibly the most striking examples; their refined colors are nearly as rich as European oil paintings. In his later works, Hokusai continued to maintain a lively interest in such styles, though he made an effort to incorporate them as naturally as possible in his work. This duality undoubtedly led to the enthusiastic response to his work in Europe; his woodcuts clearly avoid the flatness typical of earlier Japanese masters. His efforts at softening the effect of Western techniques are apparent in a later landscape of women and children collecting shells on the beach. He not only demonstrated a Western sense of perspective by drawing the figures in the foreground much larger that those further away; he also added clouds on the horizon, which he arranged in nearly hemispheric form, in accordance with his vision of the roundness of the earth.

By the middle of the second decade of the nineteenth century, Hokusai had defined his own special style of drawing, and he began to articulate it, providing those who wanted to emulate his style with a series of drawing handbooks: the Hokusai manga. The direct impetus for this series seems to have come from a visit to the city of Nagoya in the fall of 1812. During his stay there, many people approached him to ask for lessons. The introduction to the first volume of the Manga states that the numerous sketches made during these sessions were later compiled, organized and reworked by his students. The publication of this first volume in 1814 was such a success that what was originally conceived of as a single volume was extended into a series of ten. Volumes two through ten appeared at short intervals between 1815 and 1819, and provide a panoramic view of Japanese daily life, touching upon the nature, plants, animals, Gods, history and landscapes of Japan. These volumes bear witness to the great interest Hokusai had in common people, particularly the craftsmen and their tools. He was a keen, avidly curious observer, who managed to include all kinds of seemingly minor details in his drawings.

The Manga volumes remained steady sellers and were reprinted over and over during much of the nineteenth century, although today it is extremely difficult to find an early copy in good condition. Faced with such success, Hokusai apparently acquiesced to the request of his publisher, and compiled two more volumes, which appeared in 1828 and 1834, respectively. The twelfth volume is particularly rich in comic drawings, and was no doubt a source of laughter for many generations. Volumes thirteen through fifteen were collections of sketches, only some of which were Hokusai's; in fact, the last volume was not published until 1878, long after Hokusai's death.

The popularity of the Manga volumes did not deter Hokusai from working on other projects. He produced a number of picture books, both small and large, including a variety of woodcuts. These picture books present a diversity and a realism that had no real equivalent in western art at that time, ranging from a guide to sketching based on the letters of Japanese syllabary, to a series of drawings destined for use by craftsmen (for example, on the making of combs or pipes). Understandably, when they found their way to Europe in the latter half of the nineteenth century, these books contributed to Hokusai's fame and popularity, even more than his single-sheet prints.

In 1820, the Year of the Dragon ushered in Hokusai's sixty-first year, and with it, brought a period of change. Hokusai returned to the world of amateur poets he had abandoned at the end of the eighteenth century, working seriously on the surimono woodcuts with which he had only flirted earlier. His return occasioned the commissioning of what was probably the largest series of woodcuts in the square format popular at the time: a series of thirty-six prints designed to accompany a selection of poems inspired by the theme of shells. In each of the woodcuts, a shell is presented in a fan-shaped scroll. Hokusai loosed his vivid imagination, drawing in free association with the name of the shell or with the

poetry printed on the page. In the years that followed, Hokusai was to become one of the foremost artists in this medium, which was now even more elaborate than it had been several decades past. Some of Hokusai's finest still lifes date from this period.

Though now a well-respected artist in his sixties, Hokusai was not content with what he had accomplished, despite the success of his Manga series and the overall popularity of his work. In his autobiography of 1834, he wrote: "By the age of fifty, I had already published an infinite variety of drawings, but none of the work done before I turned seventy is really worthwhile." And perhaps, in a sense, he was right because his best work was still to come. He had a number of unfinished drawings that needed more work to bring them to their definitive form, such as that of the Great Wave with which he had first begun experimenting back in the 1790's. He also attempted, though not entirely to his satisfaction, to elaborate on his earlier experiments with Western techniques, which had produced such startling results in the two series mentioned above.

Towards the end of 1830, it appears that he approached the publisher Nishimuraya Yohachi with an idea for a series of large landscapes of Mount Fuji, which though sixty miles away from the capital, was frequently visible, especially in clear weather. The first ten drawings published included what are now considered to be the three most famous Japanese woodcuts in history — The Great Wave, Fuji in Clear Weather, and A Shower Below the Summit — and they were an immediate success. Though this is mere speculation, it may well have been Nishimuraya who suggested printing the remaining drawings entirely in shades of blue, thus capitalizing on the new stable pigment that had just become readily available. What is certain is that the publisher announced that the remaining landscapes would be printed in this way, though only nine of them have actually been located.

Even more important than this innovative use of color is the size of the undertaking. Originally titled, Thirty-six Views of Mount Fuji, it was the largest series devoted exclusively to landscapes ever to be attempted by any artist or publisher. One of the first in the full-size format to be devoted to landscapes, its publication was obviously an audacious novelty in this respect, but it also represented a considerable risk for the publisher. The most likely scenario is that the first ten drawings were published in 1830, followed by another ten in 1831, among which were those using the revolutionary new blue pigment. By 1834, forty-six drawings had been published, ten more than originally intended.

The risk taken by Nishimuraya paid off. The series was extremely well received, though certainly not because of its great diversity. In addition to the pure landscapes, like Fuji in Clear Weather and A Shower Below the Summit, in which there is almost no trace of human activity, there were drawings in which human activity features prominently in the foreground, with Mount Fuji discernable only in the far distance. Some of the drawings are almost purely Japanese in style, while others incorporate, in well-balanced and subtle ways, a blend of both Japanese and Western perspective. Most importantly, all of them exude an enduring sense of vitality.

Apparently the magnitude of the project, which required ten new drawings annually, did not daunt Hokusai, and in fact left him ample energy for other endeavors. Then in his seventies, he began to work feverishly on several new series of prints, again mostly landscapes. Two of the most important featured the provinces of Japan, one of famous waterfalls, the other of famous bridges. Both series, of eight and eleven drawings respectively, were issued while the Fuji project was still in full swing, and the two projects were connected in certain subtle ways. For example, the third group of Fuji drawings was printed with blue borders, as was the waterfall series; both the last group of Fuji drawings and the series of famous bridges featured black borders. Prints from these two series are rare, at least

compared to the larger Fuji series, though whether this is an indication that they were less popular is hard to say. However, as the lack of variation in their coloring proves, they were certainly not reprinted as regularly as the Fuji series.

The plates in these two series clearly demonstrate Hokusai's mastery of the landscape. Neither "true to life" nor fanciful, they represent Hokusai's vision of the majesty of nature. He invariably includes people in his drawings, generally pilgrims or other travelers admiring waterfalls, for example. The waterfalls themselves illustrate Hokusai's fascination with interplay between lines. One of the plates, the Ono Waterfall, is a later version of an image found in the seventh volume of the Manga series; in the earlier version, the viewpoint is nearly identical, with just one solitary traveler passing on the bridge in the foreground[1]. In the Bridge series, entitled Picturesque Views of Bridges in Different Provinces, the bridges themselves are situated in barren regions, where large sections of the landscape are obscured by mist rising from the valleys or by clouds clinging to the mountaintops. Despite the relative isolation of the landscape, Hokusai almost always incorporates some human presence, if only to give an indication of the dimensions being portrayed.

Other series of landscape prints from this period include woodcuts in smaller formats, possibly intended for those who could not afford the larger, more expensive, standard size used for the Fuji, Waterfall and Bridge series. One of these small-format series introduces a maritime theme, detailing the variety of methods for catching fish, from small-net

1. In reality, many of the images in the Manga volumes were later adapted into larger single-sheet drawings. The Manga volumes are clearly a treasure trove of sketches and ideas that inspired not only Hokusai's students, but also Hokusai himself.

fishing in shallow rapids to the deep–sea operations of the whaling industry near the distant Goto Islands. Hokusai brings the viewer inside the wave that fascinates him so. And by taking fishing as the common theme in this series, he again manages to bring together nature and the human beings who live in contact with it.

In another series of small-format prints, Hokusai portrays Edo, Osaka and Kyoto, the three main cities of Japan, in three traditional settings: covered by snow, bathed in moonlight and garbed in cherry blossoms. This triad, Snow, Moon and Flowers, sometimes called the Three Friends of the Poet, shows up again in another series of large-format prints depicting a snow scene in Edo, a moonlit vision of an Osaka neighborhood, and the flowering cherry trees of Kyoto.

In his short autobiography, Hokusai wrote that "it [was] at the age of seventy-three that [he] began to understand, in a limited fashion, the growth of plants and trees, and the structure of birds, animals, insects and fish". This understanding is illustrated by the work he accomplished in the 1830's in addition to his landscapes. In 1832, Hokusai completed an untitled series of ten large-format woodcuts on the traditional theme of flowers and birds. Strangely enough, birds figure in only two of the woodcuts, while insects have pride of place in five of them, leaving flowers the remaining three. Although this essentially Chinese theme was later adopted in Japanese painting, Hokusai was at the time breaking new ground. He chose a more Western perspective, almost as if he was observing the flowers through a telescope. His innovation was to present hitherto unnoticed details, isolated from the whole; the flowers as well as the insects and the birds are drawn in meticulous detail, similar to Western naturalists' drawings. That they have not been separated from nature is apparent in the other details, a bent petal, for example, suggesting a breeze. In his masterful representation of poppies bent by a strong wind, Hokusai evokes the composition of the Great Wave.

After providing the illustrations to numerous collections of popular poetry and literally thousands of surimono prints in the early decades of his career, it was only in the 1830's that Hokusai became more involved with classical poetry. In 1833 and 1836, Hokusai illustrated two collections of Chinese poetry from the T'ang dynasty in transla-

lation with commentaries. He did the same for Japanese translations of two other Chinese classics. One of the plates in the earlier volume of T'ang dynasty poems, which accompanied a poem by Tu Fu (712-70), depicts a man riding away from a friend into a wintry landscape, and is quite similar to a much larger, vertical print from the Poet series. This Poet series, a collection of ten prints whose full title was Mirror of Chinese and Japanese Poetry, was also published in or around 1833. Some of the woodcuts in it refer to actual poems; others illustrate episodes from the lives of famous poets.

In 1834, the last prints of the Fuji series and the ten plates in the Bridge series were published, but Hokusai had also been working on two other projects which he probably considered more important to his future as an artist: a series of woodcuts illustrating an extremely well-known Japanese anthology of one hundred classical poems, and a collection entitled One Hundred Views of Fuji. The first volume in the poetry anthology came out in the late spring of 1834. It included the short auto-biography cited above and announced his new pseudonym, Manji, literally "Ten Thousand Years". Probably, he had been wanting to use this name for several years already, but his publishers had advised him to continue working under the name of Hokusai Iitsu, the signature found on all majors works from this period.

With the publication of the One Hundred Poems anthology, he established his new signature, Hokusai Manji. In this book, subtitled As Explained by the Nursemaid, Hokusai's alter ego, a simple nursemaid, interprets the poems, losing her way in multiple misreadings and free associations, all of which serve as inspiration for Hokusai's imaginative illustrations. The human presence is accentuated more in this book than in any of the landscape series done previously: sometimes there are villagers at work or else simply peasants returning home at dusk. The publication of this series was interrupted by the severe economic crisis that hit Japan in 1835/36. Only twenty-seven of the illustrations were actually published, and of those, only three of the original drawings have been preserved. For the majority of the remaining unpublished drawings, only finished draft copies exist. Hokusai's principal publisher, Nishimuraya, apparently went bankrupt at this time, and his remaining stock of blocks and woodcuts were sold to an obscure publisher who managed to continue publishing a while longer.

The same fate nearly struck the collection One Hundred Views of Fuji. As mentioned above, the first volume was published in late spring of 1834; the second followed one year later. But, though the plates for the third and final volumes appear to have been cut already, the printing was postponed until the crisis was over. When it finally came out in the early 1840's, the book was printed in the standard size of most picture books, but was a deluxe version, reproduced exclusively in delicate shades of gray, and in accordance with the most exacting methods of the time. This implies the participation of the best engravers of the day (and no doubt the most skillful printers), each of them signing their blocks in the margin, a practice all but unheard of at the time.

What began as a pictorial history of the formation of Mount Fuji in the first volume, gradually developed into a vibrant tribute to the mountain in all its infinite variety, and in the end became a sort of vast "visual poem", the product of many years of artistic development for Hokusai. In the plate of Mount Fuji seen through bamboo, for example, the stalks all seem to imitate the slope of the mountain. Another plate shows a Dragon, a creature of both Water and Air believed to be the messenger of the Gods, ascending to the top of the mountain. Certainly, dragons had special meaning for Hokusai; as mentioned earlier, he felt that being born in the Year of the Dragon had had a propitious effect on his career. And after painting the mountain in all its splendor, Mount Fuji no doubt had special meaning for him too.

During the economic crisis of the mid-1830's, print publication came to a virtual standstill. Hokusai seems to have survived at first by selling his original drawings in the streets, and later, by retreating to the country-side. Then in his eighties, those years must have been difficult for him. Even after the crisis had passed, life was still not easy. Already a superstitious man, Hokusai took to starting every day by drawing a mythical lion, called shishi, to ward off bad luck. This ritual continued for over a year,

and the result was a series of imaginative creatures, scribbled on paper each morning, providing a bestiary of spontaneous drawings produced strictly for personal reasons. They date to the period beginning in the eleventh month of 1842 and continue through the twelfth month of 1843.

The third volume of his One Hundred Views of Fuji was finally published in 1842, but Hokusai had decided not to continue his work with woodcuts or book illustrations. In spite of his age, he had higher aspirations. He wrote: "At the age of eighty-six, I will have improved even more and by ninety I will surely have penetrated the mystery of life. At one hundred, I will have attained a magnificent level and at one hundred and ten, each dot and each line of my work will vibrate with life. Those who live long enough will see if I lie."

Hokusai wanted to accomplish his ambition through painting, rather than more woodcuts. In 1842, at the age of 83, he is said to have sent several pages of drawings gathered together in an album to one of his publishers, accompanied by a letter to which was attached his self-portrait as an old man. The letter reads: "The sketches in this volume were done when I was about forty or forty-one. A number of them are simple copies of already published drawings. After all these years, some of them could be reworked for publication. The rest — smile if you like — must be taken as immature work from the past. Cordially, Hachiemon (chop) Mangi at 83 years".

The features of the self-portrait are almost identical to those in his painting of Raiden or Rajin, the God of Thunder, done in 1847. The chop on this — and other paintings from these years — reads "Momo, one-hundred", the age Hokusai hoped to reach. However, the artist did not live that long; he died at the age of ninety, on the eighteenth day of the fourth month of 1849, pleading for "another ten years, or only five, maybe, to become a great painter, (maybe)". What is probably his last completed painting depicts a Dragon ascending Mount Fuji.

The actors: Sakata Hangoro III as Chinzei Hachirono Tametomo with a large axe and Ichikawa Ebizo IV as the monk Mongaku.

Hosoban diptych (314 x 135 mm each; 12.36 x 5.31 inches), signed: Shunro ga.
Published by Tsutaya Juzaburo, 1791. (Right) London, British Museum; (Left) Boston, Museum of Fine arts, Bigelow Collection Courtesy.

Netsuke workshop.

Picture book plate (200 x 315 mm; 7.87 x 12.40 inches), signed: Hokusai Sori ga.
From the picture book *Sandara kasumi*, published privately by the Kasumi poetry club, 1798. Chicago, the Art Institute of Chicago.

Women on the beach at Enoshima (Enoshima shunbo).

Picture book plate (254 x 380 mm; 10 x 14.96 inches), signed: Hokusai Sori ga; chops: Hokusai and Sori.
From the picture book *Yanagi no ito*, published by Tsutaya Juzaburo, 1797. London, British Museum.

A village by a bridge.

Picture book plate (235 x 374 mm; 9.25 x 14.72 inches), signed: Hokusai Sori ga.
From the picture book *Otokodoka*, published by Tsutaya Juzaburo, 1798. Cologne, Gerhard Pulverer collection.

Mountain landscape with a bridge.

Woodcut, *Surimono* format (126 x 171 mm; 4.96 x 6.73 inches), signed: Sori aratame Hokusai ga.
Privately published, 1799. Leiden, Matthi Forrer collection.

A lady looking through a telescope while her maidservant holds an umbrella.

Woodcut, *Oban* format, signed Kako ga.
From the series *Seven Elegant Bad Habits*, published by Tsutaya Juzaburo, late 1790. Yamaguchi, Uragami collection, Hagi Uragami Museum.

Tametomo and the demons at Onigashima.

Full-color painting on silk (593 x 819 mm; 23.35 x 32.24 inches), signed: Katsushika Hokusai Taito ga, with chop: Raishin, and a poem written by Kyokutei Bakin, 1811-1812.
London, British Museum.

People on an Ushigafuchi street at Kudan.

Woodcut, *Chuban* format (180 x 245 mm; 7.09 x 9.65 inches), signed Hokusai egaku.
From an untitled series of western-style landscapes, published anonymously, c. 1805. Paris, Bibliothèque Nationale de France.

Mount Fuji seen through the piers of a high bridge.

Woodcut, *Chuban* format (184 x 245 mm; 7.24 x 9.65 inches), signed: Hokusai egaku.
From an untitled series of Western-style landscapes, published anonymously, c. 1805. Boston, John Spaulding Collection Courtesy, Museum of Fine Arts.

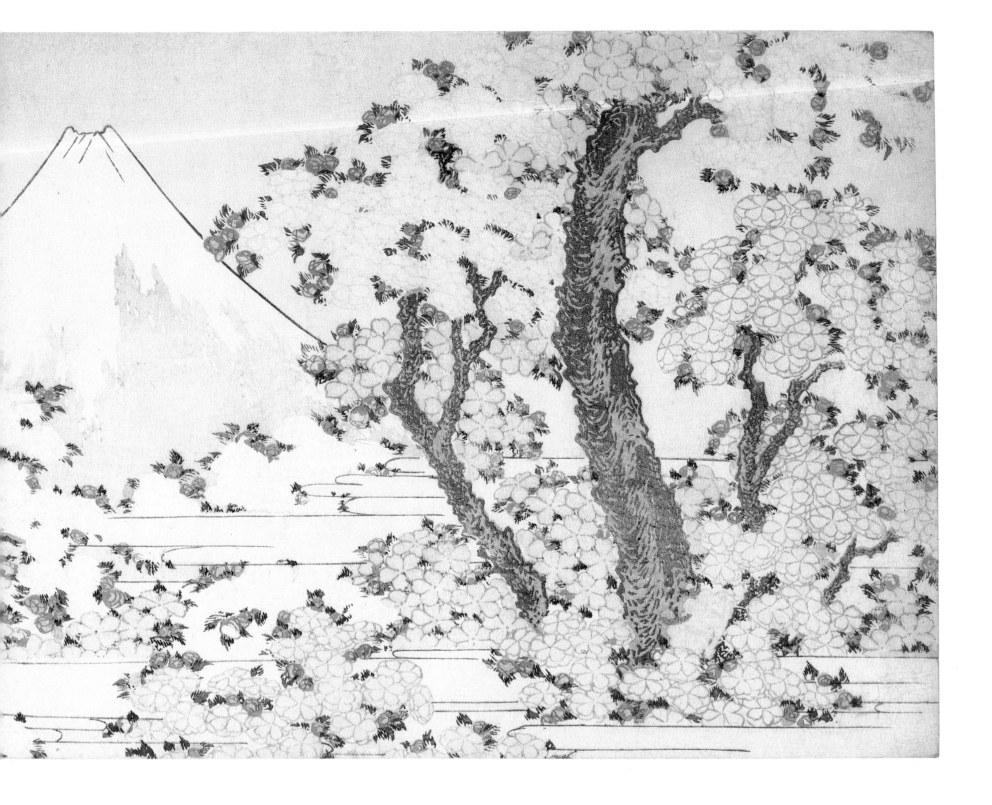

Mount Fuji with cherry trees in bloom in the foreground.

Woodcut, *Surimono* format (201 x 554 mm; 7.91 x 21.81 inches), signed: Gakyojin Hokusai ga. c. 1800-1805.
Amsterdam, Rijskmuseum.

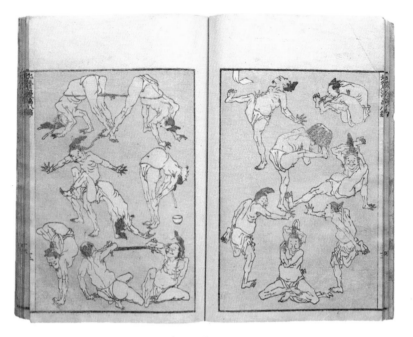

Acrobats.

Picture book plate (226 x 162 mm; 8.90 x 6.38 inches).
From the series *Hokusai manga*, vol. 8, published by Eirakuya Toshiro, 1819. Cologne, Gerhard Pulverer collection.

Fat men.

Picture book plate (226 x 162 mm; 8.90 x 6.38 inches).
From the series *Hokusai manga*, vol. 8, published by Eirakuya Toshiro, 1819. Cologne, Gerhard Pulverer collection.

Sudden wind.

Picture book plate (226 x 162 mm; 8.90 x 6.38 inches).
From the series *Hokusai manga*, vol. 12, published by Eirakuya Toshiro, c. 1834. Leiden, National Museum of Ethnology.

Philosopher watching a pair of butterflies.

Picture book plate (258 x 344 mm; 10.16 x 13.54 inches).
From the album *Hokusai shashin gafu*, published by Tsuruya Kiemon, 1814 or 1819. Leiden, National Museum of Ethnology.

Okiku, the plate specter.

Woodcut, *Chuban* format (255 x 185 mm; 10.04 x 7.28 inches), signed: zen Hokusai hitsu.
From the series *A hundred ghost stories*, published by Tsuruya Kiemon, c. 1831. Bruxelles, Musées Royaux d'Art et d'Histoire.

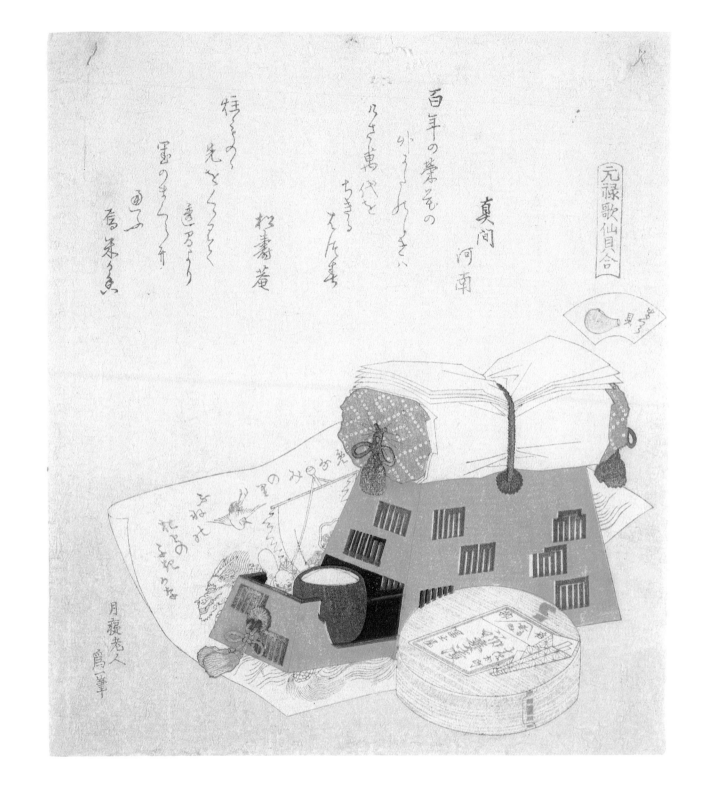

A pillow and a drawing of a Good Luck Ship (a New Year's custom).

Woodcut, *Shikishiban surimono* format (204 x 183 mm; 8.03 x 7.20 inches), signed: Getchirojin Iitsu hitsu.
From the series *A matching game the shells of the Genroku poems*, published privately by the Yomogawa poetry club, 1821. Cambridge, Courtesy of the Arthur M. Sackler Museum, Harvard University Art Museums.

A potted dwarf pine, with basin and towel on rack.

Woodcut, *Shikishiban surimono* format (206 x 183 mm; 8.11 x 7.20 inches), signed: Fusenkyo Iitsu hitsu.
From the series *A set of horses*, published privately by the Yomogawa poetry club, 1822. Amsterdam Rijskmuseum.

The warrior Hatakeyama Shigetada carrying his horse down the hill after it had been injured.

Woodcut, *Shikishiban surimono* format, signed: Fusenkyo Iitsu hitsu.
Privately published, 1822. Bergeyk, Robert Schaap collection.

Banner raising.

Paper and ink drawing, (95 x 260 mm; 3.74 x 10.24 inches), signed: Hokusai, with chop: Katsushika Hokusai.
From the picture book series, *Day and Night*, c. 1817. Boston, John Spaulding Collection Courtesy, Museum of Fine Arts.

Peasants surprised by a sudden rainstorm.

Full-color painting on Dutch paper (275 x 400 mm; 10.83 x 15.75 inches), unsigned. c. 1822-1826.
Leiden, National Museum of Ethnology.

The great wave at Kanawaga.

Woodcut, *Oban* format (255 x 380 mm; 10.04 x 14.96 inches), signed: Hokusai aratame Iitsu hitsu.

From the series *Thirty-six views of Mount Fuji*, published by Nishimuraya Yohachi, c. 1830. New York, The Metropolitan Museum of Art, H. O. Havemeyer collection, donated by Mrs. H. O Havemeyer, 1929.

A shower below the summit.

Woodcut, *Oban* format (255 x 380 mm; 10.04 x 14.96 inches), signed: Hokusai aratame Iitsu hitsu.
From the series *Thirty-six views of Mount Fuji*, published by Nishimuraya Yohachi, c. 1830. Honolulu, Academy of Arts.

Mount Fuji in clear weather.

Woodcut, *Oban* format (254 x 367 mm; 10 x 14.45 inches), signed: Hokusai aratame Iitsu hitsu.
From the series *Thirty-six views of Mount Fuji*, published by Nishimuraya Yohachi, c. 1830. Los Angeles, County Museum of Art, donated by Frederick Weisman Company.

Fuji seen from Shichirigahama Beach in the Sagami province.

Woodcut, *Oban* format (262 x 386 mm; 10.31 x 15.20 inches), signed: zen Hokusai Iitsu hitsu.
From the series *Thirty-six views of Mount Fuji*, published by Nishimuraya Yohachi, c. 1831. Dublin, Trustees of the Chester Beatty Library.

Measuring a cedar at Mishima pass in the Kai Province.

Woodcut, *Oban* format (254 x 373 mm; 10 x 14.69 inches), signed: zen Hokusai Iitsu hitsu.
From the series *Thirty-six views of Mount Fuji*, published by Nishimuraya Yohachi, c. 1831. London, British Museum.

The passenger ferry on the Sumida at Onmayagashi, with the Ryogoku bridge in the distance.

Woodcut print, *Oban* format (262 x 385 mm; 10.31 x 15.16 inches), signed: zen Hokusai Iitsu hitsu.
From the series *Thirty-six views of Mount Fuji*, published by Nishimuraya Yohachi, c. 1833.
New York, The Metropolitan Museum of Art, The Howard Mansfield Collection, acquisition of the Roger fund, 1936.

People admiring Mount Fuji from a tearoom at Yoshida.

Woodcut, *Oban* format (254 x 369 mm; 10 x 14.53 inches), signed: zen Hokusai Iitsu hitsu.
From the series *Thirty-six views of Mount Fuji*, published by Nishimuraya Yohachi, c. 1834. Leiden, National Museum of Ethnology.

People on the balcony of the Gohyakurakan temple.

Woodcut, *Oban* format (254 x 370 mm; 10 x 14.57 inches), signed: zen Hokusai Iitsu hitsu.
From the series *Thirty-six views of Mount Fuji*, published by Nishimuraya Yohachi, c. 1834. Leiden, National Museum of Ethnology.

Mount Fuji and Edo castle seen from Nihonbashi.

Woodcut, *Oban* format (262 x 386 mm; 10.31 x 15.20 inches), signed: zen Hokusai Iitsu hitsu.
From the series *Thirty-six views of Mount Fuji*, published by Nishimuraya Yohachi, c. 1834. Cologne, Gerhard Pulverer Collection.

Pilgrims at the Kirifuri waterfall in the Shimotsuke province.

Woodcut, *Oban* format (380 x 258 mm; 14.96 x 10.16 inches), signed: zen Hokusai Iitsu hitsu.
From the series *Famous Waterfalls of Japan*. Published by Nishimuraya Yohachi, c. 1832. Chicago, H. G. Mann Collection.

Woman and boy crossing a bridge (over the Tatsuta).

Preliminary sketch in black and red ink on paper for the following woodcut (266 x 384 mm; 10.47 x 15.12 inches), c. 1835.
Paris, Bérès Gallery.

Travelers on the bridge near the Ono waterfall on the Kisokaido Road.

Woodcut, *Oban* format (381 x 260 mm; 15 x 10.24 inches), signed: zen Hokusai Iitsu hitsu.
From the series *Famous Waterfalls of Japan*. Published by Nishimuraya Yohachi, c. 1838. Chicago, Art Institute of Chicago.

乳母の鑑

在原業平

千早振

弥代もきくそ

隅田川

かきりあるに

水の原とい

北斎□

The pontoon bridge at Sano in the Kosuke province in winter.

Woodcut, *Oban* format (262 x 386 mm; 10.31 x 15.20 inches), signed: zen Hokusai Iitsu hitsu.
From the series *Picturesque Views of the Bridges in Different Japanese Provinces.* Published by Nishimuraya Yohachi, c. 1832. Paris, Musée Guimet (R.M.N.).

Farmers crossing a suspension bridge on the border of the Hida and Etchu provinces.

Woodcut, *Oban* format (258 x 380 mm; 10.16 x 14.96 inches), signed: zen Hokusai Iitsu hitsu.
From the series *Picturesque Views of the Bridges in Different Japanese Provinces.* Published by Nishimuraya Yohachi, c. 1834. Chicago, H. G. Mann collection.

The raging sea at Choshi in the Shimosa province.

Woodcut, *Chuban* format (182 x 256 mm; 7.17 x 10.08 inches), signed: zen Hokusai Iitsu hitsu.
From the series *One thousand pictures of the ocean*, published by Moriya Jihei, c. 1833. Paris, Musée Guimet, R.M.N.

Moon over the Yodo river and Osaka castle.

Woodcut, *Oban* format (250 x 366 mm; 9.84 x 14.41 inches), signed: zen Hokusai Iitsu hitsu.
From the series *Snow, Moon and Flowers*, published by Nishimuraya Yohachi, c. 1833. Amsterdam, Rijskmuseum.

Bellflower and dragonfly.

Woodcut, *Oban* format (260 x 375 mm; 10.24 x 14.76 inches), signed: zen Hokusai Iitsu hitsu.
From the series *Large flowers*, published by Nishimuraya Yohachi, c. 1832. Chicago, Art Institute of Chicago.

Morning glories and tree frog.

Woodcut, *Oban* format (250 x 375 mm; 9.84 x 14.76 inches), signed: zen Hokusai Iitsu hitsu.
From the series *Large flowers*, published by Nishimuraya Yohachi, c. 1832. Chicago, H. G. Mann collection.

Poppies.

Woodcut, *Oban* format (250 x 373 mm; 9.84 x 14.69 inches), signed: zen Hokusai Iitsu hitsu.
From the series *Large flowers*, published by Nishimuraya Yohachi, c. 1832. Paris, Musée Guimet, R.M.N.

(Right) Lilies.

Woodcut, *Oban* format (250 x 370 mm; 9.84 x 14.57 inches), signed: zen Hokusai Iitsu hitsu.
From the series *Large flowers*, published by Nishimuraya Yohachi, c. 1832. Paris, Musée Guimet, R.M.N.

Two carp amidst the waterweeds.

Fan print (185 x 235 mm; 7.28 x 9.25 inches), signed: Hokusai aratame Iitsu hitsu; chop: tengu.
Unidentified publisher, 1831. Paris, Musée Guimet, R.M.N.

Two cranes on a snow-covered pine.

Woodcut, *Nagaban* format (527 x 236 mm; 20.75 x 9.29 inches), signed: zen Hokusai Iitsu hitsu.
From an untitled series of prints, published by Moriya Jihei, c. 1833. Honolulu, Academy of Arts.

The poet Li Po admiring the waterfall of Lo-Shan.

Woodcut, *Nagaban* format (519 x 231 mm; 20.43 x 9.09 inches), signed: zen Hokusai Iitsu hitsu.
From the series *Mirror of Chinese and Japanese Poems*, published by Moriya Jihei, c. 1833. Honolulu, Academy of Arts.

The poet Teba, on horseback, and his servant in a winter landscape.

Woodcut, *Nagaban* format (507 x 227 mm; 19.96 x 8.94 inches), signed: zen Hokusai Iitsu hitsu.
From the series *Mirror of Chinese and Japanese Poems*, published by Moriya Jihei, c. 1833. Paris, Musée Guimet, R.M.N.

Peasant crossing a bridge while gathering rushes.

Woodcut, *Nagaban* format (519 x 235 mm; 20.43 x 9.25 inches), signed: zen Hokusai Iitsu hitsu.
From the series *Mirror of Chinese and Japanese Poems*, published by Moriya Jihei, c. 1833. Honolulu Academy of Arts.

The poet Abe no Nakamaro gazing at the moon from a terrace.

Woodcut, *Nagaban* format (520 x 229 mm; 20.47 x 9.02 inches), signed: zen Hokusai Iitsu hitsu.
From the series *Mirror of Chinese and Japanese Poems*, published by Moriya Jihei, c. 1833. Honolulu Academy of Arts.

Fishermen hauling a net, illustration to a poem by Kakinomoto no Hitomaro.

Woodcut, *Oban* format (261 x 375 mm; 10.28 x 14.76 inches), signed: zen Hokusai Manji.
From the series *One Hundred Poems (as explained by the Nursemaid)*, published by Nishimuraya Yohachi, c. 1835. London, British Museum.

Abe no Nakamaro watching the moon from the hill, illustration to a poem by Abe no Nakamaro.

Woodcut, *Oban* format (260 x 378 mm; 10.24 x 14.88 inches), signed: zen Hokusai Manji.
From the series *One Hundred Poems (as explained by the Nursemaid)*, published by Iseya Sanjiro, c. 1835. Honolulu, Academy of Arts.

People crossing an arched bridge, illustration to a poem by Ariwara no Narihira.

Woodcut, *Oban* format (262 x 376 mm; 10.31 x 14.80 inches), signed: zen Hokusai Manji.
From the series *One Hundred Poems (as explained by the Nursemaid)*, published by Nishimuraya Yohachi, c. 1835. Chicago, Art Institute of Chicago.

Hunters around a campfire in the snow, illustration to a poem by Minamoto no Muneyuki.

Woodcut, *Oban* format (259 x 374 mm; 10.20 x 14.72 inches), signed: zen Hokusai Manji.
From the series *One Hundred Poems (as explained by the Nursemaid)*, published by Iseya Sanjiro, c. 1836. Chicago, H. G. Mann Collection.

Palanquin bearers on a steep hill, illustration to a poem by Fujiwara no Michinobu.

Woodcut, *Oban* format (254 x 369 mm; 10 x 14.53 inches), signed: zen Hokusai Manji.
From the series *One Hundred Poems (as explained by the Nursemaid)*, published by Iseya Sanjiro, c. 1835. Honolulu, Academy of Arts.

Mount Fuji seen through bamboo.

Picture book plate (227 x 156 mm; 8.94 x 6.14 inches).
From the album *One hundred views of Mount Fuji*, vol. 2, published by Nishimuraya Yohachi, 1835. Leiden, National Museum of Ethnology.

Mount Fuji and a dragon.

Picture book plate (227 x 156 mm; 8.94 x 6.14 inches).
From the picture book, *One hundred views of Mount Fuji*, vol. 2, published by Nishimuraya Yohachi, 1835. Leiden, National Museum of Ethnology.

Mount Fuji seen above the waves.

Picture book plate (227 x 156 mm; 8.94 x 6.14 inches).
From the picture book, *One hundred views of Mount Fuji*, vol. 2, published by Nishimuraya Yohachi, 1835. Leiden, National Museum of Ethnology.

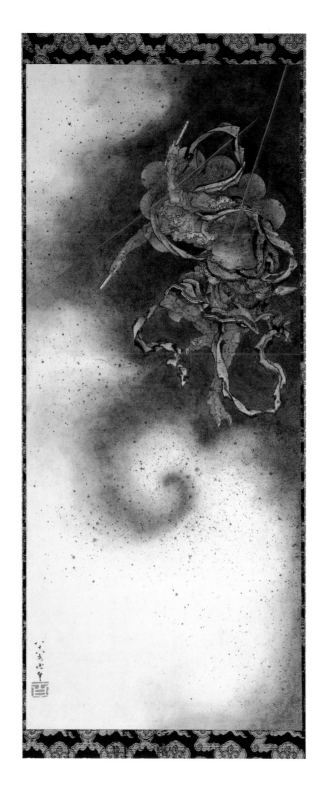

Raiden, God of Thunder.

Full-color painting on paper (1299 x 495 mm; 48.39 x 19.49 inches), signed: Manji, an old man of 88 years; chop: Momo. 1847.
Washington, Freer Gallery of Art.

Tiger in the rain.

Full-color painting on paper (1205 x 415 mm; 47.44 x 16.34 inches), signed: Manji, an old man of 90 years; chop: Mono. 1849.
Tokyo, Ota Kinen Bijustsukan.

93

Signatures

Throughout his career, Hokusai used a variety of signatures, which correspond with distinct periods. Some are simply names with which the artist signed his work; other signatures have specific meaning.

The various names used include Shunro, Hokusai Sori, Kako, Katsushika Hokusai Taito, and Hokusai.

The rough translations of those signatures that have special meaning are listed below
(The suffixes ga, egaku, and hitsu mean "drawn or done by"):

Fusenkyo Iitsu hitsu: *Iitsu, he who does only one thing.*
Gakyojin Hokusai ga: *Hokusai, crazy about drawing.*
Gakyorojin Manji: *Manji, an old man crazy about drawing.*
Getchirojin Iitsu hitsu: *Iitsu, a moon-mad old man.*
Hokusai aratame Iitsu hitsu: *Hokusai, who is changing his name to Iitsu.*
Sori aratame Hokusai ga: *Sori, who is changing his name to Hokusai.*
Zen Hokusai Iitsu hitsu: *Iitsu, formerly Hokusai.*
Zen Hokusai Iitsu: *Iitsu, formerly Hokusai.*
Zen Hokusai Manji: *Manji, formerly Hokusai.*

Japanese Woodcut Prints

The formats of Japanese woodcuts were standardized for practical reasons.
The following are the names and dimensions of the principal formats used.

Chuban: 195 x 265 mm (7.68 x 10.44 inches)
Hosoban: 330 x 150 mm (13 x 5.91 inches)
Nagaban: 530 x 236 mm (20.88 x 9.30 inches)
Oban: 265 x 390 mm (10.44 x 15.37 inches)
Shikishiban surimono: 215 x 185 mm (8.47 x 7.29 inches)
Surimono: various small formats
Tanzaku: 350 x 70 mm (13.79 x 2.76 inches)

Chop: *a design often stamped on goods in the Orient to indicate their special identity.*
Ecole Kano: *traditional Japanese School of Painting.*
Edo: *the political capital of Japan during Hokusai's life (located today in Tokyo).*
Kabuki: *Popular theater whose plays focus primarily on daily life and historical themes. Men wearing traditional make-up play all the roles.*
Manga: *humoristic sketches.*
Netsuke: *a small cut gemstone, set in wood, ivory or metal, and suspended from a chest or box with a silk cord.*
Shogun: *the supreme military ruler of Japan during Hokusai's life; based in Edo.*
T'ang: *the ruling Chinese dynasty from 618 to 907.*
Ukiyoe: *an artistic trend popular from the end of the 17th century to the end of the 19th century which, using the medium of woodcuts and illustrated popular novels, celebrated the actors of the Kabuki stage and the beautiful courtesans of the Yoshiwara district.*
Yoshiwara: *the district of Edo famous for its beautiful courtesans.*